THINGS I WANT
To SAY at WORK
But I'll
Get Fired

This Book Belongs To

Name :

Phone No :

B.C GRAHAM
PUBLISHERS
ISBN: 9789693292664
PRINTED IN THE USA

To my coffee machine – for the endless cups that fueled late nights, the patience it showed when I forgot the water, and the wisdom to never talk back. This book is as much your creation as it is mine.

Finally, To the one who truly understands me, my dog, who sat on my keyboard and added the final 'bark' to this book.

Introduction

"Things I Wanna Say At Work But I'll Get Fired"

If you've ever sat in a meeting and imagined yourself shouting what you really think, then you're holding the right book. This is your guide to all the things you wish you could say out loud at work but can't if you want to keep your job. We all have moments of frustration, whether it's because of an overbearing boss, a coworker who doesn't pull their weight, or the endless stream of emails. This book taps into that universal desire to speak our minds, with a twist of humor to keep things light.

Here, you'll find a collection of thoughts and reactions for every annoying work situation. Think of it as your secret weapon to maintain sanity in the face of workplace absurdity. Use it as a private outlet for your office grievances or as a way to find a shared laugh with coworkers who can relate.

This isn't about actually risking your professional reputation; it's about having a mental escape plan. So, the next time you're biting your tongue to stop from saying something career-ending, flip through these pages.

I have provided you with generic swearwords in their most basic, easy-to-use, boil-in- the-bag, chicken-in-a-basket, painting- by-numbers, plug-and-play, one-up-the- arse sort of way.

Remember, this book is for entertainment purposes only. So, read on, enjoy, and keep your job.

Happy swearing, or as the French say 'Va te tripoter'!

"

Can you drink the water here, or does it taste of piss, like your Coffee?

"

French:
L'eau est-elle potable, ou a-t-elle le goût de pisse, comme votre Café?

German:
Kann man das Wasser hier trinken, oder schmeckt es auch nach Pisse wie das Kaffee?

Italian:
Potete bere l'acqua qui, o gusto di orina come la vostra Caffè fa?

Spanish:
¿Se puede beber el agua aquí o sabe a pis como su café?

"Arsehole"

French:
Trou de cul

German:
Arschloch

Italian:
Budiùlo

Spanish:
Gilipollas

"Shut up."

French:
Ferme-la!

German:
Halts Maul.

Italian:
Chiuda la vostra faccia.

Spanish:
¡Cállate!

"Fuck off!"

French:
Va te faire foutre!

German:
Verpiss Dich!

Italian:
Vaffanculo!

Spanish:
¡Vete a tomar por culo!

"Dick"

French:
Bitte

German:
Schwanz

Italian:
Cazzo

Spanish:
Polla

"Bullshit"

French:
Des conneries!

German:
Kacke

Italian:
Stronzata

Spanish:
Y una mierda

"Bitch"

French:
Salope

German:
Schlampe

Italian:
Stronza

Spanish:
Zorra

"Bastard"

French:
Salaud

German:
Hurensohn

Italian:
Bastardo

Spanish:
Cabrón

"Cunt"

French:
Con

German:
Fotze

Italian:
Fregna

Spanish:
Coño

"Arse"

French:
Cul

German:
Arsch

Italian:
Culo

Spanish:
Culo

"Dyke"

French:
Gouine

German:
Lesbe

Italian:
Lesbica

Spanish:
Tortillera

" **Your company is like a toilet. It doesn't need a CEO, it just needs someone to flush all the shit away.** "

French:

Votre Entreprise est comme une toilette. Il n'a pas besoin d'un PDG, il a besoin de quelqu'un pour vider toute la merde.

German:

Dein Unternehmen is wie ein Klo. Ihr braucht keinen Vorstandsvorsitzender, sondern nür einen, der die Scheisse wegspült.

Italian:

Il vostro Azienda è come una toletta. Non ha bisogno di un Amministratore Delegato, esso necessità giuste qualcuno di irrigare tutta la merda.

Spanish:

Tu país es Empresa un wáter. No necesita un Director Ejecutivo sino alguien que tire de la cadena para que se vaya la mierda.

"Faggot"

French:
Pédé

German:
Schwuchtel

Italian:
Frocio

Spanish:
Maricón

"Fuck"

French:
Baise

German:
Ficken

Italian:
Scopata

Spanish:
Joder

"Bugger it!"

French:
Merde alors!

German:
Scheiß drauf!

Italian:
Maledicalo!

Spanish:
¡Me cago en la puta!

"Fur burger"

French:
Hamburger de fourrure

German:
Fellburger

Italian:
Hamburger della pelliccia

Spanish:
Conejito

"Piss"

French:
Pisse

German:
Pisse

Italian:
Piscio

Spanish:
Pis

"shit"

French:
Merde

German:
Scheiße

Italian:
Merda

Spanish:
Mierda

"Tits"

French:
Nichons

German:
Titten

Italian:
Zinne

Spanish:
Tetas

"Wanker"

French:
Branleur

German:
Wichser

Italian:
Segaiolo

Spanish:
Gilipollas

"Whore"

French:
Putain

German:
Hure

Italian:
Puttana

Spanish:
Puta

"Are you dribbling or do you have rabies?"

French:
Ruisselez-vous ou avez-vous la rage?

German:
Sabberst Du oder hast Du Tollwut?

Italian:
State gocciolando o avete rabbia?

Spanish:
¿Babeas o tienes la rabia?

"Please hide your face before I vomit."

French:
Veuillez cacher votre visage
avant que je vomisse.

German:
Bitte versteck dein Gesicht,
sonst muss ich kotzen.

Italian:
Nasconda prego la vostra faccia
prima che vomiti.

Spanish:
Por favor, tápate la cara si no
quieres que pote.

"

I think I might have stepped on something unpleasant. Yes, it's your company.

"

French:
Je pense que j'ai marché sur quelque chose de désagréable. Oui, c'est votre Entreprise.

German:
Ich glaube, ich bin in etwas unangenehmes getreten. Ach ja, dein Unternehmen.

Italian:
Lo penso ho fatto un passo su qualche cosa di sgradevole. Sì, è il vostro Azienda.

Spanish:
Me parece que acabo de pisar algo asqueroso. Ah, sí. Es tu Empresa.

"You have the brain of a cheese sandwich."

French:

Vous avez le cerveau d'un sandwich au fromage.

German:
Du hast das Hirn eines Käsebrötchens.

Italian:
Avete il cervello di un panino del formaggio.

Spanish:
Tienes el cerebro de
un emparedado del queso.

"

If you were twice as clever, you would still be stupid.

"

French:
Si vous étiez deux fois plus intelligent, vous seriez encore stupide.

German:
Und wenn du doppelt so schlau wärst, wärst du immer noch doof.

Italian:
Se foste due volte intelligenti, ancora sareste stupid.

Spanish:
Si fueras el doble de inteligente, aún serías estúpido.

"

I wouldn't touch you with a shitty stick.

"

French:
Je ne vous toucherais pas avec un bâton couvert de merde.

German:
Ich würde dich nicht mal mit 'nem beschissenen Besenstiel berühren.

Italian:
Non li toccherei con un bastone coperto merda.

Spanish:
No te tocaría ni con un palo lleno de mierda.

"

Your Company's quite nice, as far as leprosy colonies go.

"

French:
Pour une colonie de lèpre, votre
Entreprise est tout à fait plaisant.

German:
Für eine Leprakolonie ist Ihr
Unternehmen ziemlich nett.

Italian:
Per una colonia di lebbra, il vostro
Azienda è abbastanza piacevole.

Spanish:
Como colonia leprosa, tu
Empresa está muy bien.

"

Put a toilet on your head and keep it there while I shit on you.

"

French:
Mettez un w.c. sur votre tête et gardez-la là
tandis que je chie sur vous.

German:
Setz dir eine Toilette auf den Kopf und halt
sie fest bis ich fertig geschissen habe.

Italian:
Metta una toletta sulla vostra testa e
mantengala là mentre caco su voi.

Spanish:
Ponte un retrete en la cabeza y aguántalo
mientras yo me cago en tí.

"

You smell like a monkey's arse.

"

French:
Votre odeur est comme le cul d'un singe.

German:
Du riechst wie ein Affenarsch.

Italian:
Il vostro odore è come il culo di
una scimmia.

Spanish:
Hueles como el culo de un mono.

"

Your COMPANY is shit.

"

French:
Votre Entreprise est merde.

German:
Dein Unternehmen ist Scheisse.

Italian:
La vostra Azienda del calcio è merda.

Spanish:
Tu Empresa es una puta mierda.

"Your mother suckles pigs."

French:
Votre mère allaite des porcs.

German:
Deine Mutter säugt Schweine.

Italian:
La vostra madre allatta i maiali.

Spanish:
Tu madre da de mamar a cerdos.

"

Your mother was a hamster, and your father smelled of elderberries.

"

French:

Votre mère était un hamster, et votre père sentait des baies de sureau.

German:

Deine Mutter war ein Hamster und dein Vater roch nach Holunderbeeren.

Italian:

La vostra madre era un criceto ed il vostro padre sentito l'odore di delle bacche di sambuco.

Spanish:

Tu madre era un hámster y tu padre olía a bayas de sauco.

"

Your penis is so small that if you fucked a mouse it wouldn't notice.

"

French:
Votre pénis est si petit que si vous baisiez une souris elle ne réalise pas.

German:
Dein Schwanz ist so klein, dass es 'ne Maus nicht merkt, wenn du sie fickst.

Italian:
Il vostro penis è così piccolo che se scopaste un mouse non realizza.

Spanish:
Tu pene es tan pequeño que si te follaras a un ratón, no lo notaría.

"

Your Company is shit.

Your food is shit.

Your Coffee is shit.

I could go on...

"

French:

Votre Entreprise est merde. Votre nourriture est merde. Votre Café est merde. Je pourrais continuer…

German:

Euer Unternehmen ist Scheisse. Euer Essen ist Scheisse. Euer Kaffee ist Scheisse. So könnte ich weitermachen…

Italian:

Il vostro Azienda è merda. Il vostro alimento è merda. La vostra Caffè è merda. Potrei continuare…

Spanish:

Tu Empresa es una mierda. Vuestra comida una mierda. Vuestra Café una mierda. Podría seguir...

"I hate you!"

French:
Je vous déteste!

German:
Ich hasse dich!

Italian:
Li odio!

Spanish:
¡Te odio!

"

Go and jump off a cliff.

"

French:
Allez sauter d'une falaise.

German:
Geh und stürz dich von einer Klippe.

Italian:
Vada e salti fuori di una scogliera.

Spanish:
Ve y tírate por un precipicio.

"

I would like to

buy your Company. How much is the Shit?

"

French:

J'aime vos Entreprise.
Combien coûte le merde?

German:

Ich mag deine Unternehmen.
Was kostet der Scheisse?

Italian:

Gradisco i vostri Azienda.
Quanto è il merda?

Spanish:

Me gustaría comprarte los
Empresa.
¿Cuánto vale el mierda?

" Please stop talking loudly in that annoying language. "

French:
Cessez s'il vous plaît de parler
fort dans cette langue irritante.

German:
Hör auf, so laut in dieser nervigen
Sprache zu reden.

Italian:
Smetta prego di comunicare fortemente
in quel linguaggio irritante.

Spanish:
Por favor, deja de hablar tan alto en ese
idioma tan molesto.

"Are you inbred, by any chance?"

French:
Êtes-vous inné, peut-être?

German:
Bist du zufällig ein Produkt von Inzucht?

Italian:
Lei si sono uniti tra consanguinei, forse?

Spanish:
¿Eres así de nacimiento?

"I have you down as a bit of pigeon-licker."

French:
Je vous avez pris pour un lèche de pigeons.

German:

Ich wette du bist ein Taubenlecker.

Italian:
Li scommettevo lecco i piccioni nel vostro tempo di ricambio.

Spanish:
Te machaco.

"

Is that a suntan or do you have

shit on your fingers?

"

French:
Est-ce que c'est un bronzage ou avez-vous de la merde sur vos doigts?

German:
Bist du braungebrannt oder hast du Scheisse an den Fingern?

Italian:
È quello un suntan o avete merda sulle vostre barrette?

Spanish:
¿Eso es moreno o es que tienes mierda en los dedos?

"I don't give a shit"

"

Happy swearing!

"

Made in the USA
Middletown, DE
24 February 2024